BIRCHTOWN

and the Black Loyalists

Wanda Lauren Taylor

NIMBUS
PUBLISHING

Nimbus Publishing Limited
3731 Mackintosh St, Halifax, NS B3K 5A5
(902) 455-4286 nimbus.ca

Printed and bound in Canada

NB1165

Interior design: Jenn Embree
Cover design: Heather Bryan

Library and Archives Canada Cataloguing in Publication

Taylor, Wanda Lauren, author
Birchtown and the Black Loyalists / Wanda Lauren Taylor.
Includes bibliographical references.
Issued in print and electronic formats.
ISBN 978-1-77108-166-5 (pbk.).--ISBN 978-1-77108-167-2 (pdf)

1. Blacks—Nova Scotia—Birchtown—History—Juvenile literature.   2. Birchtown (N.S.)—History—Juvenile literature. I. Title.

FC2349.B56T39 2014   j971.6'2500496   C2014-903174-2
                                                     C2014-903177-7

Nimbus Publishing acknowledges the financial support for its publishing activities from the Government of Canada through the Canada Book Fund (CBF) and the Canada Council for the Arts, and from the Province of Nova Scotia through Film & Creative Industries Nova Scotia. We are pleased to work in partnership with Film & Creative Industries Nova Scotia to develop and promote our creative industries for the benefit of all Nova Scotians.

FSC
MIX
Paper from responsible sources
www.fsc.org   FSC® C103113

This book is dedicated to the many Black Loyalists who persevered and overcame tremendous obstacles; to the descendants who carry the stories and the legacies in their hearts; to those who continue on their quest for knowledge about this part of Canada's history; and to the spirit of those Black Loyalists who lost their lives during the struggle.

They needed to know that their lives had worth, that better days were coming for their children, and that the path they paved would open many doors for the thousands who came after them.

Table of Contents

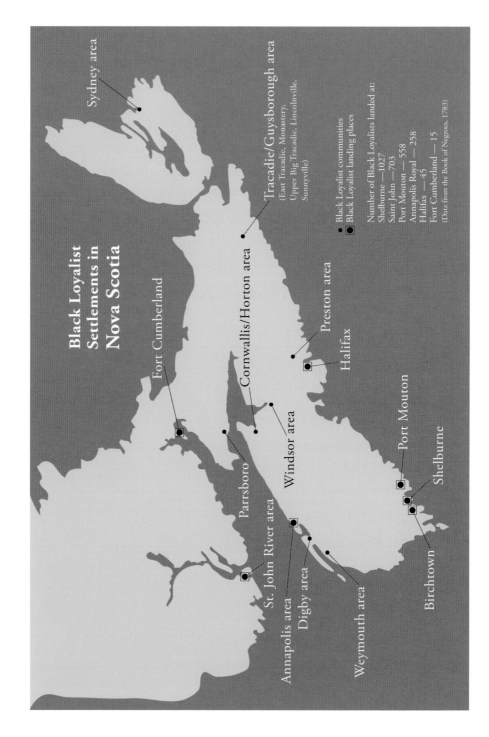

Black Loyalist
Settlements in
Nova Scotia

Sydney area

Tracadie/Guysborough area
(East Tracadie, Monastery,
Upper Big Tracadie, Lincolnville,
Sunnyville)

Fort Cumberland

Cornwallis/Horton area

Preston area

Halifax

Windsor area

Parrsboro

Port Mouton

Shelburne

St. John River area

Annapolis area

Digby area

Weymouth area

Birchtown

• Black Loyalist communities
�। Black Loyalist landing places

Number of Black Loyalists landed at:
Shelburne —1027
Saint John —703
Port Mouton — 558
Annapolis Royal — 258
Halifax — 45
Fort Cumberland — 15
(Data from the Book of Negroes, 1783)

Birchtown and the Black Loyalists

Introduction

Who Were the Black Loyalists?

Where Birchtown Began

This road runs through the centre of the Birchtown community.

If you leave the city of Halifax, Nova Scotia, and drive south for about two and a half hours, you will eventually come to a quiet little community called Birchtown[1], which began as a small Black community. It sits just a few kilometres to the south of Shelburne, Nova Scotia, and stretches along the shores of the Atlantic Ocean. When you get there, you can learn about an important story in Canada's history, and its connection to the United States and Africa.

1   Check the glossary on page 64 for all the words you see in green

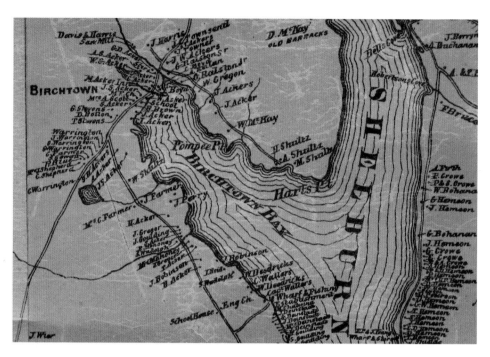

This is a map of Birchtown one hundred years after it was settled by the Black Loyalists. The map includes the names of landowners as well as some important landmarks.

The history of Birchtown began at the start of the American Revolutionary War of 1775. At that time the British ruled the colonies in what is now called America. The war began in Massachusetts that year, and it looked like the British were losing.

As colonies became more rebellious, the governor of Virginia, Lord Dunmore, offered freedom to any slave or indentured servant who would desert his or her master and side with the British in the war. These people would become known as Black Loyalists.

In 1776, thirteen united colonies declared themselves free of Britain, and the war became more intense. On July 4, 1776, leaders of these united colonies sent a letter to the King of England, called the Declaration of Independence, asking to be separated from England. They wanted to be their own country. But the British wouldn't allow it.

British Colonies

In the mid-1700s, the land that is now Canada and the **settlements** along the east coast of what is now America were all ruled by the British. These settlements were called colonies. Colonies were formed by groups of people who left their own country to settle in a new land.

At the time of the Black Loyalists, thirteen British colonies wanted to be independent: New Hampshire, Massachusetts, Rhode Island, Connecticut, New York, New Jersey, Pennsylvania, Delaware, Maryland, Virginia, North Carolina, South Carolina, and Georgia. After the war, they would form the United States.

British colonies that did not rebel against Britain included Nova Scotia (which then included New Brunswick), Prince Edward Island, Newfoundland, and Quebec, as well as East and West Florida.

Even after losing the war, Britain kept its promise and gave **Certificates of Freedom** to Black Loyalists in New York City. In 1783 over 20,000 Loyalists boarded ships leaving New York. About 3,500 were Black Loyalists or indentured servants. Some came along as the property

Evacuation Day

November 25, 1783, is known as Evacuation Day. It marked the day when British rule left what was now called the United States. On that day, Americans in New York raised their flag to celebrate as the British and Loyalist troops left in ships bound for other places, including Nova Scotia.

of White Loyalists, but most were former slaves who had earned their freedom by fighting in the war or supporting the British soldiers. Some Black Loyalists were headed to places like England and Florida, but most of them were headed north, to Nova Scotia. They were looking forward to enjoying their freedom. They had high hopes for themselves and their families in their new home.

Evacuation Day was the beginning of a new chapter for the Black Loyalists, and the end of a gloomy past. But what the Black Loyalists thought was a dream would end up being more like a nightmare for many of them.

Birchtown and the Black Loyalists

Chapter 1
The Promise of Freedom

Even though the Black Loyalists came to places like Nova Scotia on ships that left the United States, it is important to understand how they ended up in the United States in the first place. They did not go there by choice.

The Middle Passage

During the 1500s, on the west coast of Africa, most families belonged to various kingdoms, like the Benin and Yoruba kingdoms. They spoke in different languages and dialects. Unfortunately, at this time, many Africans captured other Africans and sold them to European slave traders in exchange for goods. The Europeans would bring the captured Africans back to their colonies in the West, where they would sell them for money. Those who captured the Africans did not care if they took a mother from her baby, or a man from his family.

Once captured, the Africans were chained together by their feet and necks, and were made to walk for many kilometres. Then they were taken to slave forts, also

Bance Island

The British slave-trading post with the greatest connection to North America was located on Bance Island (now called "Bunce Island"). It is a small island in the Sierra Leone River, the largest natural harbour in West Africa. Many of the captives loaded aboard slave ships at Bance Island were taken to South Carolina and Georgia. Rice was the staple crop in those colonies, and African farmers from the Sierra Leone region were well known for their rice-growing skills.

Shown above is a plywood model of the ruins made by British surveyors in 1947. It's on display in the Sierra Leone National Museum in Freetown.

called trading posts, such as Bance Island. The captured Africans would be chained there for weeks, months, and sometimes up to a year, waiting to be transported West.

Trading in slaves became a major business that happened in three steps. The first step (1–2) of the

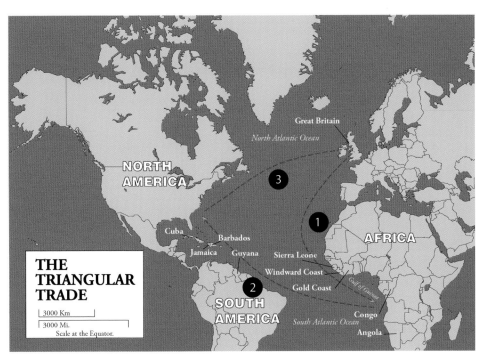

The Triangular Trade, showing steps 1 to 2, 2 to 3, and 3 to 1. The section between steps 1 and 2 became known as the Middle Passage.

slave trade would see ships leaving Europe filled with supplies like cloth, tools, and rum, and arriving on the West African coast. The second step (2–3) involved the Europeans trading those supplies for the captured Africans. The Africans were crammed into ships for the journey known as the Middle Passage, which went from West Africa to the southern colonies of what is now the United States. Conditions on the ships were so horrible that these starved captives felt ill and countless numbers

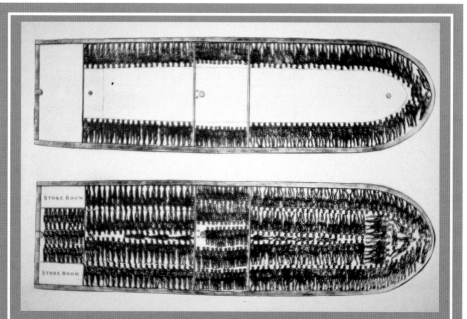

Plan of a Slave Ship

This diagram of a slave ship shows how Africans were often crammed into the bottom of ships after being captured, and then taken across the ocean to the southern colonies of what is now the United States. Those who got sick or died were tossed overboard.

of them died. Others became sick from the smells of the dying. Once the ships arrived in the New World, the third step would see the Africans traded again for supplies such as tobacco and lumber. While the Africans were put up for sale as slaves on an auction block in the colonies, the ship, filled with tobacco and sugar, would return to Europe and the first step would begin again.

Birchtown and the Black Loyalists

The Africans were frightened when they reached this new land. They didn't know English and were not allowed to speak their own languages. This rule was put in place to make sure the slaves couldn't come together to plan an escape. The slaves missed their families and did not know what would become of them once they arrived on plantations to work.

They felt depression, anger, and fear. They did not understand why they had been taken away from their lives and the people they loved, or what they had done to deserve to live as slaves among strangers. They

Some of the captured Africans were forced into slavery in sugar cane fields when they arrived in the southern colonies.

must have always wondered about their families back home in Africa. They must have wanted to see them, talk to them, and let them know what was happening. The families of the slaves must have worried and suffered, wondering what

Human Rights

We know today that the idea of keeping another human being as a slave is wrong, immoral, and cruel. Each of us, as human beings, has the right to live in a world where we are free to make our own choices. Sadly, in certain parts of the world, people continue to be enslaved. But there are community activists around the world who fight for the rights of those who become enslaved, don't have a voice, or are unable to protect themselves. For example, the United Nations works to protect the human rights of all people around the world.

happened to their mothers, fathers, sons, daughters, sisters, or brothers, who were snatched away from them so violently.

Life Before the Promise

Slaves were strangers to each other. They lived all over the British colonies, mostly on White-owned plantations. They were forced to work very hard, from sunrise until sunset. Most slaves worked in large cotton fields picking cotton from low, thorny bushes. There was normally a man, called an "overseer," watching them work. If the slaves stopped working or didn't pick enough cotton, they were punished. There were also house slaves. They did all the housework, like their master's cooking and cleaning. The slaves never received any pay for their work. Stereotypes divide slaves into these two groups: field workers and house slaves, but many also lived in town and were skilled workers, from blacksmiths to carpenters to tailors, to weavers, cooks, and herbal doctors.

> RAN away from her Master JOHN ROCK, on Monday the 18th Day of August last; a Negroe Girl named *Thursday*, about four and an half feet high, broad sett, with a Lump above her Right Eye: Had on when she run away a red Cloth Petticoat, a red Baize Bed Gown, and a red Ribbon about her Head. Whosoever may harbour said Negroe Girl, or encourage her to stay away from her said Master, may depend on being prosecuted according as the Law shall direct. And whosoever may be so kind to take her up and send her home to her said Master, shall be paid all Costs and Charges, together with TWO DOLLARS Reward for their Trouble.
>
> JOHN ROCK.
>
> HALIFAX, Sept. 1st, 1772.

This is a notice written in Halifax that offered a reward to anyone who could find a runaway slave named Thursday. Although many people believe that slavery did not exist in Nova Scotia, this document proves that it did.

One of the hardest things for many slaves was that their children were slaves too. Parents had to watch as their children were beaten, mistreated, or even killed by their masters. Parents felt helpless, because trying to protect their children meant that they, too, would be punished.

This scene shows a slave auction. Slavery existed in what is now Canada, including the buying and selling of slaves. It would not be made illegal until 1833.

Towns regularly held auctions where people went to buy and sell slaves. Once bought, slaves were considered to be a piece of their master's property. The slave would serve all his life for his or her master. And when a slave owner wrote his will, he would leave his slaves to his wife or children, along with his other possessions, like his furniture and livestock. Sadly, this meant many slaves never knew what it was like to be free.

Throughout the days of slavery, many slaves found ways to gather without their masters knowing about it. During these secret meetings, slaves would pray, hold church services, discuss local news, pass messages, and even plan escape. Many slaves secretly learned how to read and write. The more they gathered and educated themselves, the more the slaves understood their horrible living conditions, and the more they plotted their escape.

Some masters made their slaves wear special inventions, like this iron horn with bells. This way, the master could hear his slaves if they tried to run away.

Indentured Servants

Even freed Blacks who were no longer slaves were often indentured as servants. In exchange for his work, the servant would get to live and eat for free. Some identured servants were glad to know they would be fed and have a place to stay, rather than struggling in the cold weather with no food or work. Others were tricked into signing a contract that they did not understand. Either way, many freed Blacks ended up spending the rest of their lives as servants, working long, long hours. A good number did not reach the end of their contracts, because of the very harsh working conditions.

Marching to War

In the mid-1700s, tension got worse between the British and the thirteen united colonies in what is now the United States. There was talk of war. The American colonists, or "rebels" as they were called, wanted to be free from British rule.

In 1775, the American Revolutionary War began. That year, the British Crown (and in particular, the governor of Virginia, Lord Dunmore) promised freedom to any American colonist who joined the British. Many slaves living in the southern colonies heard about this promise. They saw fighting in the American Revolutionary War as their chance to be free. Once a slave decided to fight behind British lines, he received protection from the British. However, slaves still legally belonged to their masters. If a slave were found, his owner would be able to capture him and force him back home.

It is estimated that tens of thousands of Blacks signed up to fight in the American Revolutionary War, and joined military troops. Most of the slaves who fought with the British were fighting for their own freedom. These Blacks became known as the Black Loyalists.

Birchtown and the Black Loyalists

This painting, called *Soldiers in Uniform*, shows different types of American soldiers. The Black soldier on the far left was a member of the First Rhode Island Regiment, a military group made up of mostly Blacks.

During the war there were several smaller regiments made up entirely of Black Loyalists. The Black Pioneers was one of them. This regiment was established in 1776. With several hundred members, it was the largest Black regiment but was not meant to fight. Its main roles included labour and minor tasks, like keeping the streets clean of wanderers. During those hard days of war, there were people stealing and causing disturbances, and many of the Black soldiers were responsible for dealing with other Blacks who were thought to be causing trouble.

Badges on the uniforms of the Black Pioneers read the words "Liberty to Slaves." Thomas Peters, who became an important leader of the Black Loyalists, was a member of the Black Pioneers. Another member was Henry Washington, the former slave of General George Washington, who became the president of the United States after the war.

A member of the Black Dragoons, a Loyalist militia group outside of Charlestown, North Carolina.

Another unit of the Black Loyalist military was the Black Brigade. They were a highly specialized group of guerrillas. The Black Brigade operated in the New Jersey area. Its members fought against and captured many American rebels. The Black Brigade eventually joined forces with a White Loyalist unit called the Queens Rangers. Together they made surprise attacks and gave the Loyalists things like food and supplies, which they needed to survive.

Members of the Queens Rangers, a group of Loyalists who fought for the British during the Revolutionary War.

In 1781 at Yorktown, Virginia, General George Washington's American army forced General Charles Cornwallis and his British army to surrender. The Americans had won the war.

This painting shows the British, who are wearing the red coats, surrendering to the Americans, wearing blue, at Yorktown. The Black soldier at the far left of the painting and Cornwallis's other Black soldiers were likely "followers of the flag."

In total, twenty thousand Loyalists (Black and White) died or were wounded in battle during the American Revolutionary War. The end of the war saw three thousand Blacks become free because of their loyalty to the British. Thousands of Black Loyalists lived in and around New York

Followers of the Flag

During the American Revolutionary War, some Black soldiers were called "followers of the flag." They carried supplies for White soldiers, found their food, secured their horses, and cleared land for them as they travelled.

African Burial Ground

In 1991 the buried bodies of about four hundred Blacks were discovered in a section of lower Manhattan. Archaeologists discovered this to be one of the largest known Black cemeteries in North America. The cemetery was filled with Blacks who were buried during the seventeenth and eighteenth centuries, including the time of the Black Loyalists. The area was declared a National Historic Landmark. It is now the site of the African Burial Ground National Monument, which honours the spirit of those buried there.

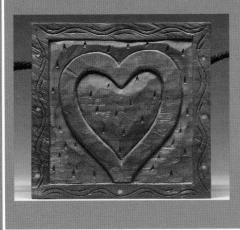

Ceremonial Coffin

This is one of the cereminial coffins used to rebury Blacks found at the African Burial Ground. It is not known for sure, but the heart-shaped design is thought to be the Sankofa, a West African symbol that means "go back and get what you've forgotten" to some. To others it means "reflecting on the past."

alone. While they waited for the new lives they had been promised, the Black Loyalists struggled to survive. Thousands lived in shacks and small shantytowns in New York. Work was scarce, and many began to worry whether the British would keep their promise and offer them new lives outside of the United States.

> ### Escape from the South
>
> When the Northern states made it illegal to own slaves in the early 1800s, many Blacks risked their lives trying to escape from their masters in the South. They would flee to the North and never look back. Some slaves were quickly caught and brought back to the South. They were punished for trying to run away and often forced back into slavery, or killed. But many slaves successfully made their way to freedom in areas like Manhattan in New York.

They waited for a long time, and the British did eventually keep their promise. But this freedom was not exactly what the Black Loyalists had hoped for, and not exactly what the British had promised.

Chapter 2

Journeys and Arrivals: Nova Scotia & West Africa

Arriving in Nova Scotia

Beginning in April 1783, Black Loyalists left New York Harbor on ships bound for British colonies, like Nova Scotia.

To board the ships, each Loyalist had to show papers proving that he had sided with the British. The Loyalist would then receive a Certificate of Freedom. The British kept a record of every person who boarded

An illustration of one of the many Black Loyalist families who came to places like Nova Scotia following the American Revolutionary War.

Certificate of Freedom

The "passport" needed to board a ship for Nova Scotia was a small paper Certificate of Freedom. Each certificate had a Black Loyalist's name on it, and said that he had sided with the British and earned his right to freedom. This is one of the few original Certificates of Freedom that still exist. It belonged to Cato Ramsey.

> NEW-YORK, 21 April 1783.
>
> THIS is to certify to whomſoever it may concern, that the Bearer hereof Cato Ramsay a Negro, reſorted to the Britiſh Lines, in conſequence of the Proclamations of Sir William Howe, and Sir Henry Clinton, late Commanders in Chief in America; and that the ſaid Negro has hereby his Excellency Sir Guy Carleton's Permiſſion to go to Nova-Scotia, or wherever elſe he may think proper. ——
>
> By Order of Brigadier General Birch,

the ships: their name, age, body type, and the names of their children. This was all written down in a record book called the Book of Negroes. This book lists each of the 1,336 Black Loyalist men, 914 women, and 750 children who boarded ships from New York to Nova Scotia, the names of the ships that carried

This painting shows Loyalists arriving in Nova Scotia. Between 1783 and 1787, close to forty thousand White and Black Loyalists settled there.

Birchtown and the Black Loyalists

them, as well as the names of their masters and the year of each Black Loyalist's escape.

By 1783, over two hundred ships carrying thousands of Loyalists had left New York Harbor. Some went to places in Europe, like England and Germany, but most of

Book of Negroes

Even though the Black Loyalists had Certificates of Freedom, there was a lot of money to be made by people called slave catchers. These people found ways to trick Black people and send them back to the United States. To avoid the slave catchers, some Black Loyalists changed their names. But today, people trying to trace their Black Loyalist family history find it difficult.

Even though some of the entries are missing a last name, the Book of Negroes has helped many Black Loyalist descendants discover their ancestors. You can see a copy of the Book of Negroes at the Black Loyalist Heritage Museum in Shelburne, Nova Scotia.

them headed north to Nova Scotia, and many arrived at Shelburne, Nova Scotia. Because families were separated during those troubling times of slavery, war, and emigration, many Black Loyalists never saw their relatives in the United States ever again.

As ship after ship pulled in to the shores of Nova Scotia, including Fort Cumberland, the St. John River area, Annapolis area, Halifax, Port Mouton, and Shelburne, Black Loyalists and their families stepped forward, not sure what to expect in this new land.

Some of the Black Loyalists moved to or stayed in towns like Annapolis Royal and Halifax. However, most of them came to the town of Shelburne and formed a settlement outside it. The Black Loyalists and those in charge decided to call this new settlement Birchtown, after British

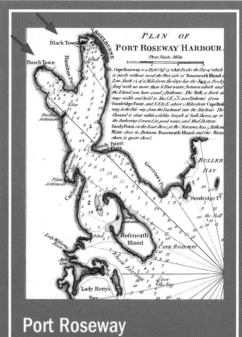

Port Roseway

Many of the Black and White Loyalists who sailed to Nova Scotia entered through Port Roseway. About a year after Loyalists arrived there, Governor Parr renamed the town "Shelburne" after the British Prime Minister, Lord Shelburne. As you can see on this map, the area included Birchtown and a small suburb called Black Town. Black Town was founded by Blacks in 1784 who were escaping the race riots in Shelburne.

General Samuel Birch. He had helped many Black Loyalists get their Certificates of Freedom in New York.

Birchtown would become the largest settlement of free blacks at that time in North America.

When the Black Loyalists first arrived in Shelburne County, most did not receive their land right away. When they did, the land they were given was far outside of

This makeshift hut, or pit house, would have been used by a family of Black Loyalists as temporary shelter while they waited for their free land.

Birchtown. The Whites who were in charge received their land and supplies first. Next were the rest of the White Loyalists and their families. Black Loyalists were last. As time passed, the Black Loyalists continued to wait for the land and supplies promised to them. Because they had nowhere to live, they were forced to move into the woods or build temporary huts called "pit houses" to protect themselves from the weather.

Each pit house was simply a roof, made of logs, poles, and branches connected together, which was placed over a large hole dug in the ground. The hole was used as a pit to make fires to keep people inside the hut warm. Black Loyalists slept on dirt floors, which they covered in fir boughs and weeds. Another fire pit outside of each hut was used for cooking and heating water.

The Nova Scotia government left the Black Loyalists to take care of themselves. Some important Blacks wrote letters to the British Crown, asking the English government to give the Black Loyalists what they had been promised. But most Black Loyalists were not given any land. And those who did receive land did not get what they were promised.

When Black Loyalists were finally given small plots of land in Birchtown, there were a few problems. The land in Birchtown was nothing but rocks, trees, and thick bushes. To add to that, the land did not officially belong to them. In order to claim ownership of their land, the government said the Black Loyalists had to clear it, get the soil ready for planting, and build at least one structure on it, like a house or a barn.

The Black Loyalists were shocked and disappointed. Without the proper tools, it was almost impossible to clear the ground to create a settlement or to grow food. Since most of them had very little or no money, they were not able to buy supplies. Even worse, many of the Black Loyalists arrived too late in the season to begin planting

Leaving Birchtown

Many Black Loyalists left Birchtown and Shelburne in hopes of finding jobs and better opportunities. Like the family in this painting travelling along the Bedford Basin, the Black Loyalists went to other parts of the province. Many left on foot.

Some Black Loyalists moved to small towns like Liverpool, Digby, and Yarmouth. Others packed up their few belongings and travelled in the opposite direction, ending up in counties such as Halifax and Guysborough.

crops. Then, in 1787, a terrible famine hit Nova Scotia, including Birchtown. Boston King wrote that people were starving in the streets, and many had to sell what they owned just to get food. There would be a lot of hard work ahead for the Black Loyalists.

The Birth of Birchtown

Some Black Loyalists worked very long hours for very little pay in the town of Shelburne. At the end of a long workday they left their jobs and walked a far distance in the other direction to the forested area where they lived. When they could, they worked to clear away what trees and thick brush they could manage.

This routine caused the Black Loyalists to become troubled and exhausted. Many of them became discouraged with all the work they had to do to own their land. They believed that the Nova Scotia government was failing them.

In 1788 about 184 Black Loyalists and their families each received thirty-four acres of land in the wooded

Birchtown school

By 1785, Black Loyalists wanted their children to have an education, so they established a small school. The teacher's name was Stephen Blucke. He taught many Black children of all different ages in a one-room schoolhouse. Stephen Blucke was one of the leaders among the Black Loyalists and was in command of the Shelburne Black Militia. He was very well educated, and had never been a slave. He fought for justice and equal treatment for all Black Loyalists.

The Birchtown school didn't last long because there weren't enough children to attend. After eleven years, the school was closed for good.

This is one of the first images of an African Nova Scotian, doing one of the few jobs held by residents in Shelburne: cutting firewood.

Black Loyalist Archaeology

Black Loyalist Archaeology was the name of a dig started in 1993 that uncovered some of the history of the first settlers at Birchtown. Scientists collected items and information from Birchtown to find out what life was like for the settlers. They found items such as pieces of earthenware (a type of old clay pottery) and a pair of scissors. The scissors probably belonged to a seamstress or a tailor (someone who makes and repairs clothing), as many Loyalists did that kind of work.

area known as Birchtown and in parts of Shelburne. Although nowhere near the two hundred acres they were each promised, it was better than nothing. The rest of the Black Loyalists continued waiting, but never received any land at all.

Shelburne Riots

During the Shelburne riots, many Blacks who lived in the town of Shelburne fled to the outskirts and into Birchtown. Birchtown residents welcomed these Blacks into their small settlement. One example is a popular preacher named David George, who fled to Birchtown after being badly beaten during the Shelburne riots. He was immediately taken in and accepted by the community.

The Black Loyalists began to face the harsh reality of their new lives in Nova Scotia. The province was not accepting of them like they had hoped. The laws in the United States were often copied in Canada, which meant that Black people in Nova Scotia were segregated from society at this time, and were not allowed to enter certain businesses. They were often called names and beaten by Whites.

Hard times fell upon the town of Shelburne and there weren't many jobs. Disagreements between Blacks and Whites increased. Many Whites grew angry because they felt the Blacks were taking the few jobs that existed. At that time, people in Nova Scotia were arguing over

Birchtown and the Black Loyalists

even the lowest-paying jobs just to be able to feed their families. These disagreements led to the Shelburne riots, which saw the Black Loyalists badly beaten and their modest homes and very few belongings set on fire.

New Hope in West Africa

Around this time, the Committee for the Relief of the Black Poor was created to help poor Blacks in London, England. Many of these poor Blacks were Black Loyalists who had fought for the British during the war. They had been sent to England at the same time other Black Loyalists were sent to Nova Scotia. They had also received the same promises of freedom, land, and supplies. However, just as the hopes of the Black Loyalists in Nova Scotia were shattered, the same thing had happened to the Black Loyalists taken to England. Many newly freed slaves in England also ended up in the streets like Nova Scotia's Black Loyalists, poor and homeless.

The Committee was created by British abolitionists, like Granville Sharp and Thomas Clarkson, who wanted to help the Blacks in England. Sharp and Clarkson thought that the poor Blacks would be happier if they could return to the continent their people had been taken from: Africa. In 1787 the Committee formed a settlement of free Blacks in Sierra Leone, called Granville Town. Among them were many of London's poor Blacks.

A portrait of Granville Sharp from his memoir, published in 1820.

Granville Town was fully formed in West Africa by 1788. It was the first town in what was called the Province of Freedom. But the settlement soon failed. There was a lack of supplies, and many arguments and misunderstandings. The language differences between the Africans and the new settlers made things worse. They argued about who owned the land that was settled by the Blacks from London. Eventually, the settlement was destroyed by the Africans. Less than three years later, disease and abandonment caused the fall of this new town.

Birchtown and the Black Loyalists

In 1790 the former Black Pioneer Thomas Peters travelled from Nova Scotia to London to speak to the British government. He demanded that the British government honour its promises to the Black Loyalists. In London, Peters met up with other abolitionists who were concerned about the treatment of Blacks. One of those abolitionists was Granville Sharp. Granville Town had just been destroyed, but Sharp wanted to form a new colony in Sierra Leone. It would be a land of promise for Blacks who had been taken from Africa. Granville Sharp felt a new hope when he met Thomas Peters. It was a chance to start again with a new group of Blacks. In 1791 the Sierra Leone Company was formed.

Sierra Leone

When Thomas Peters returned home to Nova Scotia he told other Black Loyalists about the Sierra Leone Company. He tried to convince Black Loyalists to come to a new colony in West Africa. John Clarkson was a recruiter too. He was the brother of Thomas Clarkson, the abolitionist who helped form the Committee for the Relief of the Black Poor.

A statue of Thomas Peters in Sierra Leone.

Birchtown and the Black Loyalists

They first thought they would try to convince a few hundred Black Loyalists to go to Sierra Leone, but that number quickly grew to over a thousand. These Black Loyalists wanted to leave behind their rough circumstances and the broken promises of Britain. Leaving Nova Scotia seemed right to many of the Black Loyalists, because Africa was their true home. It was the home their grandparents had been forced to leave as slaves. It was the home where they never got to live.

This is an advertisement for Black Nova Scotians to settle in Sierra Leone, from August 2, 1791. The Sierra Leone Company agreed to receive free Blacks into its colony in Sierra Leone if they could provide proof of their good character.

This map shows the coast of West Africa and the country of Sierra Leone. Black Loyalists established Freetown in Sierra Leone after leaving Nova Scotia.

Peters and Clarkson spent almost a year recruiting and planning the voyage. It would be a difficult journey across the Atlantic Ocean. It would take up to three months in rough waters, in all kinds of weather.

In 1792, almost ten years after they'd first arrived in Nova Scotia, about one-third of the Black Loyalists

Birchtown and the Black Loyalists

were ready to set sail for their new colony in West Africa. First, they had to go to Halifax and wait for the ships that would transport them across the ocean.

By mid-January of 1792, John Clarkson led over 1,100 freed Blacks to Sierra Leone. The ships were overcrowded, and many of the passengers, including Clarkson, suffered from an illness called typhoid fever. The ships arrived in Sierra Leone about two months later. It was recorded that three babies were born and about sixty-five Black Loyalists died on board before the ships reached their destination.

When the Black Loyalists arrived in West Africa they called their new colony Freetown. But things were not as they had expected. They thought there would be roads, structures, and land for them to use. What they witnessed

This watercolour painting shows what Freetown may have looked like in the early days.

reminded them of when they arrived in Shelburne. There was a lot of thick forest, a limited amount of supplies, and bad weather, including tornadoes and heavy rains. Once again, the Black Loyalists felt like they had been lied to.

But the Black Loyalists were determined, once again, to make their new life work. Life in Freetown was still much better than returning to the cold, harsh weather and treatment they left behind. Eventually, the hard work and perseverance of the Black Loyalists paid off. Even though many other groups now call

The Cotton Tree

The Cotton Tree is an historical symbol of freedom for those settlers who arrived in Sierra Leone from Nova Scotia. It is believed that this tree, which still sits in the centre of Freetown, was where the Black Loyalist settlers ran to pray and give thanks for safe deliverance to their new land.

Freetown their home, there is still a small population of Nova Scotian Black Loyalist descendants living in West Africa. These descendants help keep the history of the Black Loyalists alive.

Chapter 3
Retracing History

The Spirit of Birchtown

The Black Loyalists were survivors. They were the descendants of a group of people who were determined to succeed. Out of the Black Loyalists came some great leaders, hard workers, and strong families. Their stories are brave and powerful. Even though they faced many challenges as a people, the Black Loyalists made a permanent mark on the fabric of Canada. That means they created a legacy. Their story is a very important part of Canadian, American, and African history.

Today there are very few direct descendants of Black Loyalists still living in Birchtown. Many left for Sierra Leone and some moved to other parts of Nova Scotia, like Preston and Halifax. A lot of

These gates are the entryway into the sacred Birchtown burial ground of Black Loyalists who did not survive the harsh conditions of their new land.

the land in Birchtown was abandoned or purchased by others. But even though the descendants of Birchtown's original settlers are now spread out across the globe, their connections to each other are still very strong.

Spirituality got Black Loyalists through some of their most challenging times. During the days of slavery, it helped Black men, women, and children find the strength to survive. Many American Blacks had become Christian. They used their religion as a form of strength, and carried that strength with them as they made their way North, towards what is now Canada. They

Birchtown and the Black Loyalists

continued to practice their beliefs after they arrived, as did the Black Loyalists who returned "home" to Sierra Leone, West Africa.

Even when they were suffering, there were certain values that remained strong among the Black Loyalists, including family life, pride, respect for elders, God and spirituality, hard work, and fair treatment. A strong community spirit also helped the Black Loyalists. They were thoughtful to their neighbours, took in strangers, and gave what little they had to help others. They believed that God would bless them for their good deeds.

Many Black Loyalists attended church faithfully. They believed that no matter what their situation, they could overcome anything because of their strong faith and spirituality. Through prayer, many were able to continue on, even when things didn't seem to be going their way. This does not mean that every African Nova Scotian is religious, or even spiritual. But it is the spirit of their ancestors that gave the Black Loyalists hope, power, and the will to survive situations that many of us could not even imagine.

St. Paul's Anglican Church sits in the middle of Birchtown, facing Shelburne Harbour. It was built in

St. Paul's Anglican Church in Birchtown, established in 1888.

1888, but didn't open until about eighteen years later, in 1906. The church land was originally owned by a Black fisherman named Enoch Scott. He sold his land to priests around 1888 so they could build a church. (Anna Scott, Enoch Scott's great granddaughter, still lives in the Shelburne area.) Both Black and White people attended St. Paul's church. Unfortunately, a lot of the church's records that contained information about births, deaths, and marriages were lost in a fire in 2006. Police suspected that the fire may have been started on purpose.

Birchtown and the Black Loyalists

A group of Black Loyalist descendants in the early 1900s. Behind them is the Bethel Methodist Church in Shelburne.

The Black Loyalists were mainly Baptists and Methodists, as well as Anglicans. Today, Black Nova Scotians who are members of the African United Baptist Association gather to worship and celebrate their faith. Their values have been passed down through the generations from Black Loyalist men and women who came before them.

Black Loyalist Heritage Society

In 1997 the settlement of Birchtown received Federal Heritage Designation. This means that Birchtown is an important part of Canada's history. The Black Loyalist Heritage Museum opened at the same time, to honour and remember the history of the community. The

The site of the Black Loyalist Heritage Museum.

Black Loyalist Heritage Society played a big role in establishing the museum. The society collects, documents, and preserves the history of the Black Loyalists.

Many Black Loyalist descendants can trace their ancestry back to the United States, before the ships left New York Harbor for Nova Scotia. Members of Nova Scotia's Black Loyalist Heritage Society have a passion for researching, understanding, and sharing Birchtown's history. Some Society members have a direct blood connection, which means they are related to some of the first Black Loyalists who settled in Birchtown. Arlene Butler is one of them. She traced her roots back to Joseph Hartley.

The Society's records tell us that Joseph Hartley received his Certificate of Freedom after the Revolutionary War. He sailed for Port Mouton, a small settlement just north of Birchtown, in 1784. After he arrived, the Blacks of Port Mouton suffered a great loss when the whole town burnt down in a fire. Joseph Hartley's name later appeared in the Birchtown Muster Roll. He lived in Birchtown and travelled to work as a chimney sweep, in the town of Shelburne.

Many Black Loyalist descendants honour the memory and legacy of their ancestors by visiting Birchtown and learning about their history. Others have been studying

Birchtown Monument

In 1996 the National Historic Sites and Monuments Board of Canada created a park and monument at the Birchtown burial ground to honour and remember the Black Loyalists. The memorial plaque tells visitors, "Although diminished in numbers, Birchtown remains a proud symbol of the struggle by Blacks in the Maritimes and elsewhere for justice and dignity."

and researching for years so they can trace their family trees back through the journey of the Black Loyalists. People who have lived in Birchtown for a long time say that descendants of Black Loyalists can be found living as close by as the surrounding Black communities. Some descendants live as far away as Halifax, in other cities, in other provinces in Canada, all across the United States, and all over the world.

Elizabeth Cromwell is the executive director of the Black Loyalist Heritage Museum. She says that Black Loyalists made community wherever they went. We

In the African Nova Scotian community, youth are encouraged to discover their histories by visiting the Black Loyalist Heritage Museum and exploring what life was like for the ones who paved the way for them.

know from history that this is very true. Mrs. Cromwell also explains that a lot of mixed-race Black Loyalist descendants have been found in places as far as Belgium and Australia. Historians, researchers, descendants, and other curious people have come from all over the world to explore Birchtown. Some of these visitors have been able to find proof in their family trees of how their descendants came to Nova Scotia.

Oral Histories

In African culture, oral history is very important. Many Black Loyalist descendants tell stories, passing them down from generation to generation. These stories live on through their children, and help keep the legacy of the Black Loyalists alive. A common theme in these stories is a strong sense of community, even through all of the hardships.

Brothers Lawrence and Seldon Bruce are Black Loyalist descendants who grew up in the Shelburne area. Their family has strong ties to Birchtown. When they described life in their neck of the woods, they said it was survival of the fittest. They remembered that many of the town dumps were set up right in or very near the Black communities. This was not a good thing, especially for health reasons. The brothers also described how everyone tried to make the best out of that situation. For example, there were extra army supplies and food rations that were always being discarded at the dump. The boys remembered how, as children, they and many other residents used to go to the dump and collect the sealed rations of food from the army supplies. They would also gather up the army clothing and boots left behind and

The true spirit of Birchtown is found behind the walls of the Birchtown Community Centre, called Birchtown Hall. This building is where the community gathers and celebrates events.

wear them to keep warm during the winter months. The brothers remembered that these were some of the things families had to do to survive.

Another Black Loyalist descendant is the historian Pastor Debra Hill. She wanted to discover the history of the Black Loyalists, so she became a researcher. She was one of the first researchers of records and documents on the first Black Loyalists who crossed the shores to Shelburne. Her amazing work, collecting and preserving rare documents, was destroyed in the fire that burned the original Black Loyalist Heritage Society building. But the Society's home has been rebuilt, and Pastor Hill

continues to preserve Black Loyalist history.

Whatever their situation, whatever their choices, the descendants of Black Loyalists are here because their ancestors were determined to pave a new path. No matter what problems they faced, they had strength on the inside. It was the one thing throughout their historical journey that no person could ever take away. Many people today believe that the strength and determination shown by the Black Loyalists and their descendants has continued on into other Black settlements across the province.

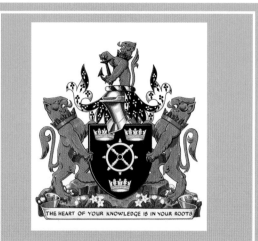

THE HEART OF YOUR KNOWLEDGE IS IN YOUR ROOTS

Coat of Arms

"The heart of your knowledge is in your roots." That is the motto for the coat of arms for the Black Loyalist Heritage Society. The wheel represents the past and the ships bringing the Loyalists to their new home. It also represents the present, the community steering towards one goal. The lions represent the Black Loyalist soldiers and are also a symbol of the courage and pride of Africa.

Important Birchtown Residents

Colonel Stephen Blucke

Stephen Blucke was born a free Black around 1752 in Barbados. He moved to New York City just before 1770, then served as colonel in the Shelburne Black Militia, and later went on to teach at the Birchtown school up until it closed in 1796. He was one of the few leaders who urged the Black Loyalists to remain in Nova Scotia and not leave for Sierra Leone. He was a leader among the Black Loyalists.

David George

David George was born into slavery, but escaped when he was a teenager. He helped found the the Silver Bluff Baptist Church in South Carolina. It was one of the first Black churches in North America. He was known across Shelburne for his preaching. However, he left Shelburne and fled to Birchtown after being badly beaten in the Shelburne race riots. He emigrated to Sierra Leone with many other Black Loyalists in 1792.

Boston King

Boston King was born into slavery in 1760, but escaped from South Carolina in 1780. When he arrived in Nova Scotia, he worked in carpentry and on ships. He spent the next few years preaching in Black settlements in Nova Scotia before he **immigrated** to Sierra Leone in 1782. He then studied in England, became a Methodist minister, and returned to Africa.

Sketch of Boston King.

Cato Ramsey

Cato Ramsey and his wife were slaves who fled from Virginia with their three children in 1776. Cato was owned by a Dr. Ramsey, while his wife and children were owned by Matthew Godfrey. Both plantations were near each other. After Cato and his family escaped to British lines and received their Certificates of Freedom, his wife, China, changed her name to Jane and took Cato's last

Birchtown and the Black Loyalists

name, Ramsey. Cato's Certificate of Freedom is one of the few originals that still exist today (see page 22). It can be viewed at the Black Loyalist Heritage Museum and other African Canadian historic locations.

Thomas Peters

Thomas Peters was a slave from North Carolina who served with the Black Pioneers. He became a sergeant and was transported from New York to Nova Scotia after the war. Peters was also one of the leaders who influenced Black Loyalists to leave Nova Scotia and travel to Freetown, Sierra Leone. He travelled across Nova Scotia telling Loyalists about the new settlement, and his efforts helped to sign up even more Blacks than the Sierra Leone Company thought they could. He is often called "The True Founder of Freetown."

Moses Wilkinson

Moses Wilkinson was a slave from Virginia who escaped after Lord Dunmore's proclamation—an escape made all the more remarkable given that Wilkinson was blind and walked with a cane. He became a Methodist preacher at Birchtown and convinced his congregation to leave Birchtown for Sierra Leone. He was one of the greatest leaders of the Black Loyalists.

John Clarkson

John Clarkson was sent to Nova Scotia by the Sierra Leone Company in England. His job was to recruit Black Loyalists to form a new colony in West Africa. After he signed Loyalists up for the new colony in Sierra Leone, he made the arrangements for the ships that would transport them there.

Birchtown Timeline

1775 The British begin recruiting Black Loyalists to help fight against the American rebels. In exchange, the British promise these people land and a new life in places like Nova Scotia. The recruits include slaves who escaped to New York.

1782 At the end of the war, the Loyalists begin to leave by ship from New York to Nova Scotia and other areas as promised.

1783 Over a hundred ships arrive on the shores of Port Roseway, now known as Shelburne, Nova Scotia. Most Blacks eventually settled around the bay, in the place now known as Birchtown.

1784 By this time, White Loyalist settlers had received most of what they were promised (land, food, and supplies) by the British.

1784 Canada experiences its first large race riot, in Shelburne.

1785 Stephen Blucke, who can read and write, becomes the schoolmaster for the children living in Birchtown. He teaches in a one-room schoolhouse, and is considered to be very successful as a teacher.

1787 Harsh winters, bad treatment, and poorly built shelters cause more suffering among the Black Loyalists. A famine occurs across the province. More people die. Provisions do not make their way to anyone.

1792 The Sierra Leone Company offers a new life to Black Loyalists and an opportunity to establish a new town in Sierra Leone. Over 1,500 people leave Nova Scotia to establish the new settlement, called Freetown.

1796 After many families leave for Sierra Leone, there are very few students left to teach. Stephen Blucke's Birchtown school closes.

1796 Just over 500 Jamaicans, called the Trelawny Maroons, are sent to Nova Scotia as punishment for rebelling against the British colonial government. They settle in Preston on what used to be the lands of the Black Loyalists who moved on to Sierra Leone. The Maroons lived among and intermarried with the Loyalists who stayed behind. Many were sent to help build the Citadel fortress.

1800 The Maroons become frustrated that the Nova Scotia government is using them for cheap labour. Nearly all of the Maroons leave Halifax for Sierra Leone.

1812 War breaks out between the United States and Britain, leading to the freedom of over two thousand former slaves, called the Black Refugees.

1813 The third wave of Blacks, the Black Refugees, arrives in Nova Scotia under a British promise. What is left of Nova Scotia's Black population is isolated and scattered. The Black Refugees settle in Nova Scotia, including areas that were abandoned by the Black

Loyalists and Maroons who had left for Sierra Leone years earlier. Black Refugees go on to establish lasting and successful communities throughout Nova Scotia.

1830s A White schoolmaster named Roswell Brown, who moved to Birchtown from New York, starts a one-room schoolhouse on his land.

1833 Slavery is abolished by the British Parliament.

1864 Rose Fortune, a famous Black Loyalist descendant who lived in Annapolis Royal, dies in February at the age of ninety. She was known for operating her own business, moving supplies and goods, and acting as a police officer. It is believed she came to Nova Scotia on a Loyalist ship after the American Revolutionary War, when she was a small child.

1888 Members of the Birchtown community begin construction of St. Paul's Church on land sold to them by a Black fisherman named Enoch Scott.

1906 Saint Paul's Anglican Church opens in Birchtown.

1960 Birchtown Consolidated School is built. Today, the building serves as the museum for the Black Loyalist Heritage Society.

1993 Birchtown is the site of an archaeological dig led by Laird Niven. This marks the first time in Canada an archaeological dig is conducted for a Black settlement. Artefacts such as glass, earthenware, and flint (a form of mineral) are found.

1993 The African Burial Ground in New York is designated a National Historic Landmark and a New York City Landmark.

1994 There is another archaeological dig at Birchtown. This one is led by Dr. Stephen Davis and archaeologists from St. Mary's University Field School. They uncover a pit house.

1996 The National Historic Sites and Monuments Board names Birchtown a national historic site. The Board builds a monument there that tells the story of the Black Loyalists' arrival in Nova Scotia in 1783.

1996 The Black Loyalist Heritage Society acquires St. Paul's Church when it buys land to build its heritage site.

1997 The Black Loyalist Heritage Society acquires Birchtown's one-room schoolhouse, built in the 1830s.

1997 Two more archaeological digs in the community of Birchtown confirm that it is a historical site. One dig uncovers what is believed to be the site of military leader Colonel Stephen Blucke's house.

1998 Over three thousand artefacts are uncovered from an archaeological dig in Birchtown.

1998 The Black Loyalist Heritage Society receives a Volunteerism and Multicultural Award from the Province of Nova Scotia for their work in preserving history.

2000 The Black Loyalist Heritage Society opens the Black Loyalist Museum, located in the Old School House. The over three thousand artefacts are preserved at this site, along with an exhibit from the Nova Scotia Museum, called "Remembering Black Loyalist Communities."

2002 The Boardwalk and Seawall are constructed around the sacred Black Burial Ground in Birchtown. The beginnings of a Heritage Walking Trail begin to take shape.

2003 A reburial ceremony takes place for the remains of the 419 Blacks found at the African Burial Site in New York City. The remains are reburied on October 4.

2006 A suspicious fire burns down the administration building of the Black Loyalist Heritage Society, destroying many rare artefacts and historical documents important to the community. Also destroyed in the fire are the library, computers and all of the Society's information, planning documents, and furniture.

2010 Planning begins for the new Black Loyalist Heritage Centre. It will include a multi-million-dollar interpretive centre, which will be built on the land occupied by the first settlement of Black Loyalists in Nova Scotia. It will be the first centre of its kind in Canada and will display the journeys of the Black Loyalists, from Africa to the United States, to Birchtown, and, for some, back to Africa. Black Loyalist history will be explored through presentations, public-education programs, and year-round events.

2014 Construction begins on the new Black Loyalist Heritage Centre.

Today Only a few families descended from the Black Loyalists still live in Birchtown. Many left for West Africa in 1792. Over the years, some moved into Halifax, while others formed settlements across Nova Scotia. Many empty Birchtown lots have been sold, bought up, and taken over by non-Loyalists.

Acknowledgements

The author would like to extend a sincere thanks to the current and former residents of Birchtown, who shared their stories and experiences. A special thank you also goes out to those who shared their photographs for the book, both the photos that were used and the ones there wasn't enough space to use.

There are also small pieces in this book taken from my documentary *Still Here: A Journey to Triumph* (2011). These include the personal stories of some Birchtown residents and Black Loyalist descendants. A heartfelt thank you is extended to them. Their memories and passion for history continue to be shared among many.

The author would also like to thank Joseph Opala, historian and Sierra Leonean for his valuable contributions to this book. Finally, the author would like to thank all of those societies and organizations across Canada, the US, and Africa for the use of their archival materials for this book.

Glossary

abolitionists: Black and White people who did not agree with the idea of slavery. They fought to help end slavery and believed that all people should live freely and in peace.

Black Pioneers: an African corps which fought in the American Revolutionary War and then helped build the Birchtown settlement.

Black Loyalists: Blacks who sided with the British during the American Revolutionary War in exchange for freedom from slavery and poor treatment. They were sent from New York to live in British colonies, like Nova Scotia, after the war.

Black Loyalist Heritage Society: a committee of people made up of mainly Black Loyalist descendants. It promotes the history of the Black Loyalists and works towards preserving valuable documents and collections that tell their story.

Book of Negroes: a book that listed each and every Black Loyalist who boarded the ships from the New York after the American Revolutionary War.

British Crown: another way to refer to British Royalty and the Queen, which are the symbols of British power.

Certificate of Freedom: paper certificates earned by Blacks who fought against the American rebels on the side of the British before November 30, 1782. These certificates confirmed a Black person's right to travel to, and live and work anywhere.

descendants: offspring or children who can trace their blood lines back to a specific generation or period.

dialect: a form of language or speech that is known and understood by a particular group of people.

emigration: the act of leaving your country to go and live in another.

guerrillas: small independent groups who participate in fighting against larger groups. Guerillas are usually fighting for freedom or for some greater cause.

immigration: when people arrive at, or relocate to a new land. Black Loyalists immigrated to places like Nova Scotia after the American Revolutionary War.

indenture: a legal contract that involves a person (White or Black) agreeing to act as a servant to another, for a period of years. During the contract, the servant could not leave their job or refuse to work. In return they were promised shelter, food, clothing, and medical attention. These contracts could be sold without any say from the servant, meaning that indentured servants were often sent to other areas, away from their families.

New World: refers to North and South America, particularly when Europe was exploring and colonizing these areas.

plantation: a very large farming estate.

proclamation: a declaration or announcement made by a government about a law, policy, or societal rule.

provisions: supplies that the government provided to families, such as flour, potatoes, and other items they needed in order to survive.

regiment: a military unit or large group of troops, usually commanded by an officer. A regiment usually has several battalions, or divisions, who provide service and protection in wartime.

settlement: a place where a group of people decide to build shelter, and live and work together.

shantytown: a series of shacks situated close together that provides a form of shelter for people living in poverty.

slavery: the practice of one human "owning" another as their property. This means the person who is enslaved has to serve their owner, has no rights, does not have the freedom to live as they choose, and is often misreated, sometimes brutally.

Recommended Reading

Kositsky, Lynne. *Rachel: Certificate of Freedom.* Toronto: Penguin Canada, 2003.

Livesey, Robert, and A. G. Smith. *The Loyal Refugees.* Toronto: Stoddart Kids, 1999.

Robart-Johnson, Sharon. *Africa's Children: A History of Blacks in Yarmouth, Nova Scotia.* Toronto: Natural Heritage, 2009.

Sadlier, Rosemary. *Leading the Way: Black Women in Canada.* Toronto: Umbrella, 1994.

———. *The Kids Book of Black Canadian History.* Toronto: Kids Can, 2003.

Smith, Craig M. *The Ultimate African Heritage Quiz Book: Maritime Edition.* Halifax: Nimbus, 2008.

Warner, Jody Nyasha. *Viola Desmond Won't Be Budged!* Toronto: Groundwood, 2010.

Wesley, Gloria Ann. *Chasing Freedom.* Black Point, NS: Roseway Publishing, 2011.

Image Credits

Nova Scotia Museum: 23, 52

Shelburne County Museum: 43

Library Archives Canada: 27, 29 (top), 45

Black Cultural Centre: 21

Black Loyalist Heritage Society: 25, 29 (bottom), 39, 46, 50

Don Troiani, historicalimagebank.com: 16, 17

Anne S. K. Brown Military Collection, Brown University Library: 15, 18

National Park Service, African Burial Ground National Monument: 20

Bridgeman Art Gallery: 8, 9, 22, 37

Library of Congress: 4

Nova Scotia Archives: 2, 11, 12,, 22, 24, 35

Joseph Opala: 6

Wanda Taylor: 1 (left), 42, 44

Bonnie Williams: 1 (right), 36, 38, 40, 49

Canstock: 38 (top), 40

Emmanuel King on behalf of the Krio Descendants Union London: 34

Wilson Special Collections Library University of North Carolina at Chapel Hill: 12

Index